D.H. La
& Cornwall

ISBN 978 185022 228 6

Published by Truran, Goonance, Water Lane, St Agnes, Cornwall TR5 0RA
www.truranbooks.co.uk

Truran is an imprint of Truran Books Ltd

Designed by Alix Wood, www.alixwood.co.uk

Printed and bound in Cornwall by R Booth Ltd, The Praze, Penryn, TR10 8AA

Cornish Lives

D.H. Lawrence
& Cornwall

Philip Payton

The Road to Rananim

We go to Cornwall, on Thursday. There is the beginning.

SO WROTE D.H. LAWRENCE on Monday 27 December 1915, in a letter to his friend Lady Ottoline Morrell, the celebrated aristocratic hostess of Garsington Manor in Oxfordshire. It was wartime, and although there would be yet worse to come – the Somme, Passchendaele and other cataclysmic struggles all lay ahead – it was apparent already that the Great War was not going well for Britain and that, even if it could be won, the cost in lives and human misery would be huge.

Lawrence had already made a name for himself in the literary world, and moved in influential circles, his friends and correspondents including society figures such as Ottoline Morrell and Lady Cynthia Asquith. Several of his poems had appeared in the prestigious *English Review* in 1909, and his first novels *The White Peacock* (1911), *The Trespasser* (1911) and *Sons and Lovers* (1913) had all been well received, even if they were not yet making him much money. Yet behind this veneer of success and a fast-growing reputation, Lawrence was not a happy man.

For Lawrence, the Great War was a tragedy beyond measure, and it was this that drove him to Cornwall – and 'out of England'. There was also the complication of his recently acquired German wife, Frieda, cousin of Baron Manfred von Richtofen, the 'Red Baron' ace so accomplished in the shooting-down of Allied airmen. Ottoline Morrell thought Frieda 'aggressively German', as she noted in her journal in June 1915, with Lawrence 'crushed and unhappy' as a result of her rages and outbursts. 'Poor Lawrence', Ottoline wrote, 'what a distraught creature he is underneath'.

But Lawrence's anguish ran deeper than his tempestuous relationship with his wife. The war was the culmination of his disappointment with England. Born into a working-class family in the coal-mining town of Eastwood, Nottinghamshire, in 1885, Lawrence wrote at length in his short stories and novels about the lives of ordinary people, professing not only to understand them but to love them too. Yet he also thought working-class life 'dark and violent', as he told Ottoline Morrell in his letter of 27 December. The working classes were 'passionate enough', he said, 'sensuous, dark – God, how all my boyhood comes back – so violent, so dark, the mind always dark and without understanding. It makes me sad beyond words. These men, whom I love so much.' Pausing for a moment, he added: 'I love them like brothers but, my God, I hate them too'.

The only thing the working people understood now, he complained to Ottoline in his letter, was 'industrialism, only wages and money and machinery. They can't *think* anything else...They are utterly unable to appreciate any pure, ulterior truth: only this industrial – mechanical – wage idea'. To this debasement by the forces of industrialisation, as Lawrence saw it, was added the war itself. He had witnessed the formidable German Army exercising in Bavaria before the outbreak of hostilities, and knew at once that any future conflict would be murderous and destructive on a grand scale. As he had observed in the *Manchester Guardian*, this would be industrial warfare: 'a war of machines, and men no more than the subjective material of the machine'. And so, as he was to write later in his novel *Kangaroo*, 'It was in 1915 the old world ended. In the winter of 1915-16 the spirit of the old London collapsed...and became a vortex of broken passions, lusts, hopes, fears, and horrors'.

Lawrence's disillusion with England was made all the more complete in 1915 by the banning of his latest novel *The Rainbow* on the grounds of obscenity, leaving Lawrence low in spirits and short of cash. Philip Morrell, Ottoline's husband and a Liberal MP, spoke in the House of Commons in support of the book's publication, to no avail. By now, Lawrence had already begun to think of abandoning England – at least metaphorically, and if possible physically too – by creating somewhere an alternative utopian community of like-minded spirits. This would be his *Rananim* – a whimsical, romantic name, possibly of Hebrew origin, that he had borrowed from one of the lyrical 'Russian' songs on the lips of his friend, Samuel Koteliansky, a Jewish-Ukrainian émigré that Lawrence had met on the eve of the outbreak of war in 1914. Koteliansky – or 'Kot' as he was known to Lawrence and other close friends – was extremely supportive of Lawrence during those difficult war years. It was a constancy that Lawrence thought to be bravely emblematic of the *Rananim* ethos, and he and Kot maintained an intimate correspondence that lasted until just weeks before Lawrence's death in March 1930.

At first, casting around for a home for his proposed *Rananim*, Lawrence thought to take up Philip Morrell's offer of renovating a building on the Garsington estate, only to find that refurbishment costs made this unrealistic. Thereafter, with the ever-increasing desire to turn his back on

Middleton Murry with Frieda and D.H. Lawrence on their
wedding day, 13 July 1914 (TOPFOTO)

England, Lawrence looked further afield, becoming more expansive in his ambitions. As Ottoline noted in her journal, he 'said he must leave England, and go to a country that has a future before it, a country that is in the spring of its life. Here in England the autumn has set in, life is dead, the land dead, the people are dead sapless sticks'. And so, she wrote, 'He is determined to go off to America and write for Americans'. She could hardly agree with his pessimistic assessment but concluded that 'it will be better for him to go to fresh fields than to stay here bemoaning and wailing the decay of England, especially as his health is very bad'.

Lawrence and Frieda by now had the offer of a cottage at Fort Myers in Florida, and were scraping together the funds to make the journey. Lawrence had also made friends with a young musician, Philip Heseltine, whom he hoped would join his *Rananim* community, and Heseltine was at that very moment in correspondence with the composer Frederick Delius about the possibility of settling on his ramshackle estate, also in Florida. The plans seemed to be coming to fruition. But then Lawrence made a mistake. To be given permission to go to America, he would need a medical certificate exempting him from military service on the grounds of ill-health. Given his weak chest, this was surely a formality, and Lawrence attended a medical board in London in December 1915. He waited his turn for hours but, just as he was nearing the head of the queue, he panicked and fled. Without his exemption, he could not cross to America, and so Florida was put on hold for the moment. But he needed desperately to get out of London, and his friend, the novelist J.D. Beresford, suggested kindly that he move for the time being to his holiday home at Porthcothan on the north coast of Cornwall, near Padstow. Gratefully, Lawrence accepted, writing in his letter to Ottoline Morrell that Cornwall would be the first step on the road to *Rananim*: 'Cornwall and Florida; the germ of a new era'.

'I Like Cornwall Very Much.
It Is Not England.'

D.H. LAWRENCE WAS NOT the first to find in Cornwall an 'otherness' that allowed him – as he imagined it – to escape the oppressions of everyday life, and to find renewal and a sense of freedom rekindled. He certainly would not be the last. As Denys Val Baker, author and literary critic, wrote much later in 1973, 'It would be difficult to drum up much romantic excitement about "going to Essex" or "going to Bucks" or "going to Leicestershire" – yet even to this day there remains an intangible yet very real romanticism about "going to Cornwall"'. As he concluded: 'It is going west, towards the sun, into another world'. This is what Lawrence wanted, and the chance offer in late 1915 of a Cornish sojourn unveiled for him the opportunity to try to wrest free from all that oppressed him in metropolitan England – or so he thought. If not exactly 'the original New Age traveller', he was, as Alan M. Kent has observed, an early forerunner of 'those who have flocked to Cornwall to escape urbanity throughout the twentieth century by constructing alternative lifestyles'. As Lawrence himself had explained to Lady Cynthia Asquith, writing to her the day before Christmas Eve 1915, 'Beresford has lent us his house near Padstow, on the sea in Cornwall. Some members of our Florida expedition are coming too – we begin the new life in Cornwall. It is real'.

Years after, Ottoline Morrell mused on the trauma that had sent D.H. Lawrence to Cornwall in December 1915 – and later to France, Italy, Ceylon, Australia, America, Mexico. 'The War shook, him', she said, 'the War and a very anti-English wife made him turn away in despair. His reaction against England...was the passionate reaction of hurt feelings. His whole attitude to England was that of someone who has loved and has been hurt, bruised and disappointed'. Cornwall was not America but also, as Lawrence was quick to point out, 'It is not England'. Writing to his agent, J.B. Pinker, from Porthcothan on 1 January 1916, just a few days after his arrival, he mused on the psychological distance between Cornwall and the London he had now abandoned, and on the healing power of Cornwall itself. 'Already, here, in Cornwall, it is better', he wrote, 'the wind blows very hard, the sea all comes up the cliffs in smoke. Here one is outside England...it is better in Cornwall'. Two days before, the night he and Frieda had arrived, he had written to his friend Kot. 'My dear Kot', he explained, 'This is the first move to Florida. Here already one feels a good peace and a good silence, and a freedom to love and to create

D.H. Lawrence, taken by Lady Ottoline Morrell, 29th November 1915
(NATIONAL PORTRAIT GALLERY, LONDON)

a new life'. But there was still urgency beneath this apparent serenity, a plea not to lose sight of the *Rananim* goal: 'We must begin afresh – we must begin to create a life all together – unanimous. Then we shall be happy. We must be happy'.

A few days later and Lawrence got around to writing to his new landlord, J.D. Beresford. 'We have been here a week', he said, 'so I must report myself to you'. He enthused: 'We *love* being here...The house is always peaceful and a real delight'. He and Frieda had already begun to explore the locality. 'We have walked to Padstow', he explained, 'and to the next bay north – and to-day right up on the downs, looking upon the country, upon St Columb and beyond Wadebridge'. This growing familiarity with the topography of the hinterland encouraged Lawrence's awakening sense that Cornwall itself might indeed be his *Rananim*. 'I do like Cornwall', he told Beresford:

> It is something like King Arthur and Tristan. It has never taken the Anglo-Saxon civilization, the Anglo-Saxon sort of Christianity. One can feel free here, for that reason – feel the world as it was in that flicker of pre-Christian Celtic civilization, when humanity was really young – like the Mabinogion – not like Beowulf and the ridiculous Malory.

Lawrence wrote to Kot the very next day, expansive now in extolling the charms of Cornwall. 'I am willing to believe there isn't any Florida', he said, 'it is very nice down here in Cornwall'. He and Frieda would be there until March, he added, after which 'I shall just go where the wind blows me, the wind of my own world'. But for the moment there was redeeming Cornwall: 'I like being here. I like the rough seas and this bare country, King Arthur's country, of the flicker of pre-Christian civilisation. I like it very much'. It was a theme he repeated to Katherine Mansfield in a letter composed on 7 January. 'I love being here in Cornwall – so peaceful, so far off from the world. But the world has disappeared for ever – there is no more world any more: only here, and a fine thin air which nobody and nothing pollutes'. Likewise, in a letter to Ottoline Morrell penned on 9 January, though complaining of the onset of one of his heavy colds (prompting Ottoline to send him a yellow woollen jersey by return), Lawrence explained that although they had only 'been here a week...I like it exceedingly. The sea rages under the black rocks, and the western sky is iridescent at evening...I have become much happier here'. Two days later and he repeated again to Catherine Carswell, the Scottish author and drama critic, what was close to becoming a mantra:

I like Cornwall very much. It is not England. It is bare and dark and elemental, Tristan's land. I lie looking down the cove where the waves come white under a low, black headland, which slopes up in bare green-brown, bare and sad under a level sky. It is old, Celtic, pre-Christian. Tristan and his boat, and his horn.

Similarly, writing to the literary duo Katherine Mansfield and John Middleton Murry on 17 January, Lawrence rehearsed once more the now familiar theme:

I still like Cornwall. The house is a big, low, grey, well-to-do farm-place, with all the windows looking over a round of grass, and between the stone gate pillars down a little tamarisky lane, at a cove of the sea, where the waves are always coming in past jutty black rocks. It is a cove like Tristan sailed into, from Lyonesse – just the same. It belongs to 2000 years back – that pre-Arthurian Celtic flicker of being which disappeared so entirely...All is desolate and forsaken, not linked up. But I like it.

Porthcothan Beach

Porthcothan House

Here the winds are so black and terrible. They rush with such force that the house shudders, though the old walls are very solid and tick. Only occasionally the gulls rise very slowly into the air. And all the while the wind rushes and thuds and booms, and all the while the sea is hoarse and heavy. It is strange, one forgets the rest of life. It shuts one in within its massive violent world. Sometimes a wave bursts wth a great explosion against one of the outlying rocks, and there is a tremendous ghost standing high on the sea, a great tall whiteness.

Letter to Ottoline Morrell, 15 February 1916

Perhaps Cornwall was *Rananim*. He urged Ottoline to visit him in Cornwall, to experience what he now felt so strongly: 'the sea on the wild coast is like the dawn of the world. Oh, it is good, there are no more Englands, no nations, only the dark strong rocks and the strong sea washing up out of the dawn of the sky. It is the beginning, the beginning only.'

'Heseltine Is Also Here'

CHARMED AND INTRIGUED BY Lawrence's vivid descriptions and his enthusiasm, Ottoline decided that she would accept his invitation to visit. But in the event she went down with an illness – as did Lawrence, whose bad cold proved to be the prelude to a full-blown bronchial attack which confined him to bed for a fortnight and frightened him (and Frieda) into thinking that he might be dying. His 'consumption' – tuberculosis – was catching up with him. Plainly, the escape to Cornwall, whatever else it was, was not an escape from ill-health, and there were limitations to what this Cornish *Rananim* – with its damp climate and chill winds – could offer.

But, although his illness contributed to a sense of borrowed time, spurring him on in his writing, Lawrence was not deterred by the experience – far from it. He continued to focus on his planned community of like-minded souls in Cornwall. Even as he lay on his sick-bed he had enjoyed the company of Philip Heseltine, whom he still considered a prime candidate and ideal partner for the *Rananim* project, and whom he had persuaded to join him at Porthcothan. Shortly to become a significant composer and music critic, Heseltine was in 1916 at the brink of a successful career. Much of his work would exhibit a 'Celtic' influence – notably his well-known *The Curlew*, a song-cycle for tenor and chamber ensemble based on four poems by the Irish writer and Celtic revivalist, William Butler Yeats. Heseltine's songs, written mostly for voice and piano, would become enormously popular in inter-war Britain, although, like Lawrence, he had a restless, contrary, self-destructive streak. He died as a result of a domestic gas leak when aged only thirty-six, although it was never established whether this was suicide or an accident.

'Heseltine is also here', Lawrence had written excitedly to Ottoline in his letter of 9 January. Philip Heseltine had not yet developed his potential as an individual, Lawrence thought – 'I like him, but he seems empty, uncreated' – yet there was promise, and 'one always believes in the miracle, in something supernatural'. Heseltine had already warmed to the notion of *Rananim*, and like Lawrence saw in Cornwall the 'Celtic other' which distanced it from degenerate England and made it an ideal location for their proposed community. Although he was born in London, Heseltine's family home was Cefn Bryntalch in Abermule, Montgomeryshire, and he had already developed an interest in the Welsh language and in Pan-Celticism. It seems likely that it was Heseltine who introduced Lawrence to the

Hasan Shahid Suhrawardy, Philip Heseltine (Peter Warlock), and
D.H. Lawrence, taken by Lady Ottoline Morrell 29 November 1915
(NATIONAL PORTRAIT GALLERY, LONDON)

subtleties and complexities of the 'Celtic world', giving content and meaning to Lawrence's otherwise vague conceptions of 'King Arthur's country' and a 'pre-Christian Celtic civilization'. Yet Lawrence had also done his own Celtic home-work, and, through his knowledge of the work of 'Mrs Henry Jenner', was almost certainly aware of the activities of the influential Henry Jenner, the celebrated Cornish language specialist who in 1904 had produced his all-important *Handbook of the Cornish Language* and was hailed later as 'The father of the Cornish revival'.

'Mrs Henry Jenner' – Kitty Lee Jenner (née Rawlings) – was a Cornishwoman, from Hayle. She had been a correspondent of Henry Jenner, the couple discovering to their delight much in common, including a penchant for ritualistic Christianity and – as Alan M. Kent has put it – a 'shared interest in the academic sphere of Celtic Studies'. Eventually, in 1877, the two were married, at St Erth in Cornwall. Soon 'Kitty Lee' (her *nom-de-plume*) was developing a successful literary career, with novels such as *When Fortune Frowns: Being the Life and Adventures of Gilbert Coswarth – A Gentleman of Cornwall*, published in 1895, the story of a Cornish Jacobite who had fought for Bonnie Prince Charlie in the 'Forty-Five'. Jenner himself was a convinced Jacobite, with links to various shadowy 'Legitimist' causes in Britain and continental Europe, and he and Kitty fashioned their own political-religious creed, combining elements of Jacobitism, Catholicism and Celticism. Kitty had also nurtured a parallel interest in Orientalism and 'the East', which in turn fed her growing pre-occupation with Christian art. She published three important books on the subject, under her name as 'Mrs Henry Jenner', the final being *Christian Symbolism* in1910.

It was this book that had caught Lawrence's attention. He was reading it avidly in December 1914, writing on or about the 19th of that month to the Irish barrister Gordon Campbell (later Lord Glenavy) to sing its praises and to recommend it as essential reading. Lawrence hoped that it would lift Campbell from his fixation with Ireland to a wider appreciation of 'the Celtic Vision' (as he called it), enabling him to 'understand the Celtic Symbolism in its entirety'. In the same letter, he had also urged that this 'Celtic Symbolism' be considered alongside the religious cultures of 'the *East*: Christian, Mohammedan, Hindu, all'. The influence of 'Mrs Henry Jenner' was unmistakeable here, as was Lawrence's emerging interest in Pan-Celticism. A month later, January 1915, and Kitty Lee Jenner's impact upon Lawrence was made even more plain in a letter to Kot. 'What about *Rananim*?', Lawrence enquired impatiently, 'Oh, we are going. We are going to found an *Order of the Knights of Rananim*'. Its badge, he explained, would be a 'phoenix argent, rising from a nest of scarlet, on a black background'. To show Kot exactly what he meant, he sketched his idea of the phoenix resurgent – an almost identical copy of the illustration of a 'Phoenix Rising From the Flames' opposite p.150 in 'Mrs Henry Jenner's' *Christian Symbolism*. Thereafter, Lawrence adopted the phoenix as his personal symbol, a lasting tribute, perhaps, to the influence of Kitty Lee Jenner and Celtic Cornwall.

Philip Heseltine was probably aware of much of this background. Indeed, while Heseltine was at Porthcothan, Lawrence was writing to Ottoline Morrell asking her to search out books for him 'on interesting Norse literature, or early Celtic, something about Druids...or the Orphic Religions, or *Egypt*, or on anything really African', reflecting the eclectic study he had urged on Gordon Campbell a year before. Heseltine, for his part, was bent on pursuing his own brand of Celticism. Although this came to full fruition after he had left Cornwall – following his stay at Porthcothan and later at Bosigran, near Zennor – and when he had fled to Ireland during 1917 to avoid conscription into the Army, it was surely in his discussions with Lawrence that his ideas on the place of Cornwall in the Celtic world had first taken firm shape. Indeed, the relationship between Lawrence and Heseltine was at that moment critical for both men, and it is useful to pause briefly to consider the impact of Cornwall (and thus Lawrence) upon Heseltine's own life and work. As the Scottish composer Cecil Gray was to write, Heseltine had conducted:

a comprehensive comparative study of all the various branches of the Celtic languages – Irish, Welsh, [Scots] Gaelic, Breton, Manx and Cornish...he obtained as thorough a knowledge of Irish as any Englishman can hope to do, and...This he acquired chiefly during a stay of two months either in Achill or in the Aran Islands...during which time he did nothing else except study the language...But the Celtic language which attracted him above all others was Cornish.

As Heseltine intimated, writing to Cecil Gray, learning Cornish had been an act of faith in Lawrence's original conception of *Rananim* – the 'mystic centre of a new culture' and an 'anti-national...protest against imperialism'. As Heseltine put it:

> *The Cornish language should be revived, nay, is being revived, for am I not myself reviving it? For many excellent reasons...All neo-Celtic nationalism is in effect anti-national, in the sense in which we detest nationality; it becomes an individualizing moment – a separating one, at any rate. What more effective protest against imperialism (in art as in other matters) could you or I make by adopting, as a pure ritual, a speech, a nationality, that no longer exists.*

Although Henry Jenner was at first dubious about reviving Cornish as a spoken language, he would have stoutly resisted Heseltine's contention that Cornish 'nationality' no longer existed. No matter; he and Heseltine embarked on a collaboration that would see at least one of Jenner's Cornish-language poems put to music by Heseltine. Heseltine was fast emerging as a composer of distinction. His earliest surviving orchestral work, *An Old Song*, was probably begun in Cornwall in 1916 and completed in Ireland a year later. It was intended originally as part of a *Celtic Triad*, together with a *Dirge* and a *Cornish Rhapsody* that was later destroyed. As Heseltine wrote to a friend in August 1917 from County Kerry, 'The tune is Gaelic but the piece for me is very much the Cornish moor where I have been living. The tune should emerge, as from afar, chiming in with one's thoughts while walking...a mood half-contented and half sad'.

Next was *A Cornish Christmas Carol*, composed in 1918 but not published until 1924, the second of two carols on which Heseltine had been working. 'The music of these carols is inseparably associated with the actual Cornish words', he insisted, 'any translation would pervert the whole character of the works'. As he explained to Cecil Gray, 'I am writing with great enthusiasm two Cornish hymns: it is probably the first time the old language has ever been musicked deliberately...it is wonderful for singing purposes, containing many sounds almost unknown in English (except Cornish-English dialect) which have a real musical value of their own'.

The *Cornish Christmas Carol* created something of a sensation in the Celtic world, the Breton commentator Paul Ladmirault in 1927 eulogising Heseltine as 'one of the greatest English composers of our time' and heaping praise on that 'peal of all the carols, a *Cornish Carol* for four voices, on a text in the old Cornish language, dead [sic] sister of Armorican [Breton]'. Yet the first of Heseltine's two *Kanow Kernow* (Songs of Cornwall) was not published until as late as 1973, being the music to words written by 'Gwas Myhal' (the bardic name of Henry Jenner). Entitled *Benneth Nadelik ha'n Bledhen Noweth* (Christmas and the New Year Blessing), the piece was simpler than the earlier carol but included a pronunciation glossary to help choirs unfamiliar with the Cornish language. It was, in its way, an unforeseen but lasting outcome of the *Rananim* quest, and of Heseltine's complex relationship with both Lawrence and Cornwall.

'Peter Warlock'

TOGETHER AT PORTHCOTHAN, D.H. LAWRENCE and Philip Heseltine no doubt shared their knowledge of the Jenners – Kitty Lee and Henry – swapping notes on the Celtic revivalism that had become so apparent in Cornwall, and accommodating this vision within their own conception of *Rananim*. However, there was a further dimension to Heseltine's Cornish-Celtic enthusiasms, and this was his fascination with the occult. Re-inventing himself as 'Peter Warlock', Heseltine had come under the spell of Aleister Crowley, famously dubbed 'the most wicked man in England'. Crowley was a member of the Hermetic Order of the Golden Dawn, a secret magical order which, in the late nineteenth and early twentieth centuries, had a deep impact upon western occultism. It attracted several prominent Celtic revivalists to its ranks, including the Irish nationalist and 'Celtic Twilight' writer William Butler Yeats and the Welsh novelist Arthur Machen, author of *The Great God Pan* (1894) and *The Secret Glory* (1922), a book which greatly influenced the young John Betjeman.

Likewise, Aleister Crowley was an associate of L.C.R. Duncombe-Jewell, the Cornish-Celtic revivalist who in the early 1900s had been a leading luminary of the revivalist Cowethas Celto-Kernuak – the Cornish-Celtic Society – of which Henry Jenner was also a prominent member. Moreover, Crowley had found himself in tune with much of Jenner's philosophical thought, attracted as he was by 'what they called the Celtic Church' and 'the quest of the Holy Grail', and becoming 'a romantic Jacobite...a bigoted legitimist'. But increasingly Crowley lent towards paganism and supernatural magic, gaining his infamous reputation as 'the Beast 666'. There were rumours of his activities in Cornwall – of black masses on Bodmin Moor, on the Isles of Scilly and (improbably) in St Buryan church – and it was alleged that he (with his Devil-worship) was implicated in the strange and sudden death of Katherine Arnold-Foster at Tregerthen (where, coincidently, Lawrence had lived in 1916) in May 1938.

As Paul Newman has shown, it was Crowley who introduced Heseltine to drugs, especially hashish, and who urged him to find his real self or 'True Will' by seeking spiritual wisdom through the occult. By the time Heseltine arrived at Porthcothan to stay with Lawrence in early 1916, he was already something of a specialist in the occult, with an awareness of Crowley's links with Duncombe-Jewell, Jenner and the world of Cornish-Celtic revivalism. It is difficult to gauge the extent to which this particular enthusiasm affected Lawrence. But we know that Lawrence unhesitatingly described Cornwall as 'pagan' and 'pre-Christian', echoing Heseltine's conviction, a view that he was not afraid to repeat or to deploy in fictional writing. Significantly, in his seminal novel *Kangaroo* (1923), the semi-autobiographical work that forever ties Lawrence to Cornwall, his *alter ego*, Richard Lovat Summers, contemplates the essential pagan landscape of West Penwith:

> *the twilight, awesome world of the previous Celts. The spirit of the ancient, pre-Christian world, which lingers still in the truly Celtic places...The old Celtic countries never had our Latin Teutonic consciousness, never will have. They have never been Christian, in the blue-eyed, or even in the truly Roman, Latin sense of the world. But they have been overlaid by our consciousness and our civilization, smouldering underneath in a slow, eternal fire.*

Philip Heseltine
(Peter Warlock)

Rananim Deferred

As D.H. Lawrence's first real recruit to what he hoped would become his Cornish *Rananim*, Philip Heseltine had much to recommend him – artistic, musical, other-worldly, anti-war, loather of the nation-state, escapee from oppressive England, and a budding Celticist with an interest in 'pagan' and 'pre-Christian' Cornwall and in contemporary Cornish revivalism. Yet, despite their obvious intimacy and their shared goals and enthusiasms, it was soon apparent that all was not necessarily harmonious between Lawrence and Heseltine. It was the first intimation that the road to *Rananim* would be always tortuous and difficult, for close-quarter communities would surely breed their own disagreements, quarrels and jealousies.

To begin with, Heseltine had not come to Cornwall alone. He had brought with him his already pregnant girlfriend 'Puma', Minnie Lucy Channing, sometimes also known as 'Bobby', one-time model of Augustus John. With a reputation for sexual promiscuity and a volatile temper, Puma was bound to set nerves jangling at Porthcothan. She was thought to be 'exotic' and 'exceptionally beautiful', and the artist Adrian Allinson, who had introduced Puma to Heseltine, described her as 'Italian-like, feline...fierce'. Heseltine had been captivated by her laugh, said Allinson, 'She was Philip's ideal woman – dark, with fur all over her'. And he added: 'a puma, of course, is a feline beast of prey'.

At Porthcothan, there were already signs of tension between Heseltine and Puma. Lawrence confided to Ottoline Morrell in his letter penned on 13 January 1916 that Heseltine 'says he despises her [Puma] and can't stand her, that she's vicious and a prostitute'. But, wrote Lawrence, 'She's not so bad, really'. Indeed, he added, 'I'm not sure whether her touch of licentious profligacy in sex isn't better than his deep-seated conscious, mental licentiousness. Let them fight it out between them'. Heseltine's love life, it turned out, was even more tangled than it had at first seemed, and Lawrence and Frieda observed with some amusement his vacillations between Puma, Dorothy Warren (Ottoline's niece, now a new recruit for *Rananim*), and the Swiss governess on Ottoline's staff at Garsington who had caught Heseltine's eye, Mlle Juliette Baillot. Lawrence reported these twists and turns in his correspondence with Ottoline. 'About Heseltine and Mlle', he wrote on 15 February, 'He wants Mlle for *companionship*, not for the blood connection, the dark, sensuous relation. With Puma he has this second, dark relation, but not the first'.

When Heseltine found out that Lawrence had been speculating in letters to Ottoline about the intimate details of his private life, he was not pleased. Likewise, when it became apparent that Heseltine had himself written to Ottoline, attempting to intervene in a misunderstanding between Ottoline and Frieda, it was the Lawrences' turn to be upset. Things at Porthcothan were becoming a little tiresome. Another young recruit to the *Rananim* project had by now arrived in Cornwall, the Bulgarian writer Dikran Kouyoumdjian (Michael Arlen, as he would become), whom Lawrence thought was showing promise. But he soon decided that he did not like this loud and offensive foreigner. Nor did Heseltine. 'Heseltine is still here', Lawrence reported to Ottoline, 'But he and Kouyoumdjian are most antagonistic, so it's a bit trying'. In fact, Kouyoudmdjian had 'brought the atmosphere of London', Lawrence complained, 'most disturbing', not at all what one expected from a *Rananim* recruit. 'How I loathed that London', Lawrence added, 'that England out there'. He also wrote to John Middleton Murry and Katherine Mansfield, telling them about 'Kouyoumdjian, whom I don't care for really'. Significantly, Lawrence anticipated that 'he will go soon', intimation that membership of *Rananim* was conditional, that one would be expelled or frozen out if one did not measure up to Lawrence's standards.

The Bulgarian left but Heseltine persevered for a time, trying to put together a private publishing scheme that won Lawrence's admiration. But, as Lawrence explained to Ottoline on 25 February, Heseltine remained in a state of some agitation. He was 'in a great state of (unjustly) hating the Puma, and looking on Mlle as a white star', he wrote, and would 'oscillate violently' in his affections. 'He is really very good', Lawrence admitted, 'and I depend on him and believe in him. But he is exasperating'. However, as Lawrence acknowledged, part of Heseltine's anxiety was his fear of conscription into the British Army. '[C]onscription hangs over his head like the sword of Damocles', Lawrence explained to Ottoline, adding with an air of resignation that Heseltine would probably remain with them in Cornwall, but only 'if he escapes conscription'. The conscription issue weighed heavily on Lawrence, not only because he feared for Heseltine's future, but because its hectoring presence in Cornwall now represented the unwarranted, obtrusive influence of the England he hated. For all Cornwall's non-English attributes, the dead hand of England still held ultimate sway.

Not long after Christmas 1915, Lawrence had felt the creeping, insidious influence of England's war already making itself felt in Cornwall. Emma, the housekeeper they had inherited at Porthcothan from J.D. Beresford, was a single mother whom both Lawrence and Frieda adored. Behind her back they called her 'Cornish Pasty', more in fun than anything else, despite the pejorative overtones, while to Ottoline they were prepared to admit that she was 'a good soul...a good cook...really splendid'. Lawrence was saddened when the war intruded on Emma's simple life – and, by implication, on his own attempt to escape England's reach – writing to Beresford to explain that 'the war has come'. The locals were 'very sad', Lawrence wrote: 'Emma was telling us of her sister-in-law, who had just been stitching the armlet on her husband's sleeve', preparing his uniform for the horrors that lay ahead. 'It's come now', Emma said to Lawrence, 'We've never had it till now, but it's come now. I'm sure, when I look at these buttons', continued Emma, 'We've got the Kaiser to thank for these. Every stitch I put in goes through my heart'. This was 'rather beautiful', Lawrence thought, 'showing sincere gentleness and a power of love'. He contrasted this thoughtful Cornish maid with 'The English women [who] stitch armlets on freely enough: they have lost the power of love. But it does linger here'.

But despite his admiration for the Cornish in their passive stoicism in the face of coercion, Lawrence bridled at their inability to react, to do anything about it. Like many of his time and education, he sat uncomfortably on the cusp of two, alternative constructions of 'the Celt'. He had readily embraced the contemporary Edwardian view, the 'Celtic Twilight' picture of the Celtic peoples as dreamy, other-worldly, creative, artistic, poetic – an almost pre-Raphaelite, neo-Arthurian construction that saw the Celts as somehow ethically and culturally superior to the dull, hard-headed, unimaginative, utilitarian Anglo-Saxons, the English. In such a view, the Celts were an unsullied pre-modern people, like the 'Red Indians' of America (as Lawrence would have imagined it), pure and elemental and free from the destructive forces of modernity and industrialisation. Such were the thoughts that had drawn Lawrence to Cornwall in the first place. Yet English prejudice was not yet free of the alternative construction, born of the Irish and Highland potato famines, where the Celts were fey, feckless, even subhuman, incapable of reasoned or measured behaviour and destined for ever to remain under England's guiding rule. In his darker moments, Lawrence turned to this view. He had nothing but contempt for the Irish rebels of Easter 1916, condemning them for pouring further miseries on an already traumatised people, and he dismissed David Lloyd George as a 'Welsh *rat*'.

When the war had intruded on Cornwall so soon after his arrival, Lawrence felt somehow betrayed, that the Cornish had failed to offer their 'not of England' protection that he had anticipated. It was a rude shock, and Lawrence blamed the Cornish for their lack of moral courage, as he saw it, for their infuriating self-satisfied, introverted complacency. They had turned in on themselves, and were now only interested in money. He tried to explain his contrary feelings to J.D. Beresford, writing on 1 February 1916:

> *The Cornish people still attract me. They have become detestable, I think, and yet they aren't detestable. They are, of course, strictly* anti-social *and un-Christian. But then, the aristocratic principle and the principle of magic, to which they belonged, these two have collapsed, and left only the most ugly, scaly, insect-like, unclean* selfishness*, so that each one of them is like an insect isolated within its own scaly, glassy envelope, and running seeking its own small end. And how foul that is! How they stink in their repulsiveness.*

And yet, despite this appalling fall from grace, Lawrence argued, there were still redeeming features, a hint of the old aristocratic, magical superiority that somehow still survived in the Cornish people:

> *Nevertheless, the old race is still revealed, a race which believed in the darkness, in magic, and in the magic transcendency of one man over another, which is fascinating. Also there is left some of the old sensuousness of the darkness, a sort of softness, a sort of flowing together in physical intimacy, something almost negroid, which is fascinating.*

> *But curse them, they are mindless, and yet they are living purely for social advancement. They ought to be living in the darkness and warmth and passionateness of the blood, sudden, incalculable. Whereas they are like insects gone cold, living only for money, for* dirt. *They are foul in this. They ought all to die.*

The rant over, Lawrence added sheepishly: 'Not that I've seen very much of them – I've been laid up in bed. But going out, in the motor and

Porthcothan Beach

so on, one sees them and knows what they are like'. Yet behind his anguish, as Lawrence well knew, was the war. 'The young men are all being called up now round here', he told Beresford, 'They are very miserable. There are loud lamentations on every hand. The only cry is, that they may not be sent out to France to fight. They quite shamelessly don't want to *see* a gun. I sympathise perfectly with this'. He added, gloomily: 'The cursed war will go on for ever'.

Rananim Regained? 'The Promised Land'

COMPLAINING NOW OF D.H. LAWRENCES'S unbending, authoritarian manner, Philip Heseltine decided to bow out of *Rananim* for the time being. At the same time, Lawrence and Frieda were searching for a new home, now that their tenure at Porthcothan had almost expired. Lawrence desperately wanted to remain in Cornwall. He wrote politely to Beresford on 1 February 1916: 'I should like to stay in Cornwall. I like it so much. We might afford a cottage, I think...we are very badly off'.

Casting around for somewhere new to live, the temptation was to head still further west, towards the sun and the Atlantic and America, into the yet more remote Celtic fastness of the Penwith peninsula. On 24 February he wrote to his friends John Middleton Murry and Katherine Mansfield to say that he and Frieda had found somewhere: 'It is about 7 miles from St Ives, towards Land's End, very lonely, in the rocks on the sea, Zennor the nearest village: high pale hills, all moor-like and beautiful...very wild'. It was a wonderful spot, he said: 'Primroses and violets are out, and the gorse

Zennor Church

Tinners' Arms Inn, Zennor

is lovely. At Zennor one sees infinite Atlantic, all peacock-mingled colours, and the gorse is sunshine itself'. Indeed, 'when I looked down on Zennor, I knew it was the Promised Land, and that a new heaven and a new earth would take place...I have a sense of a new spring coming very joyful from the unknown'. It was a theme he repeated to Ottoline Morrell the next day: 'When we came down over the shoulder of the wild hill, above the sea, to Zennor, I felt we were coming into the Promised Land. I know there will be a new heaven and a new earth...we have triumphed. I feel like a Columbus who can see a shadowy America before him'. Zennor would be, he said, 'a new continent of the soul. We will be happy yet, doing a new, constructive work, sailing into a new epoch'.

Here were the high hopes of *Rananim* renewed, and Lawrence immediately set about enticing John Middleton Murry and Katherine Mansfield as his latest recruits. Although not married until 1918, the 'Murrys' (as they were known) were already a couple, and were recognised as such by friends and literary acquaintances. John (or Jack) was an author, editor and literary critic, and had worked on the staff of the *Westminster*

Gazette and *Times Literary Supplement*. Katherine, a New Zealander by birth, was already a literary figure of some standing, renowned for her short stories. In July 1914 she and John had been witnesses at the Lawrence's wedding but by early 1916 were living in the South of France. They enjoyed the countryside and the weather but Katherine had been greatly shocked by the death in October 1914 of her brother, Leslie, another victim of the Great War, and was still grieving.

Staying initially at the 'Tinners' Arms' in Zennor, while the cottage at nearby Higher Tregerthen was made ready, Lawrence wrote enthusiastically to the Murrys, explaining on 5 March that 'We have been here nearly a week now. It is a most beautiful place: a tiny granite village nestling under high, shaggy moor-hills, and a big sweep of lovely sea beyond, such a lovely sea, lovelier even than the Mediterranean'. The countryside around Zennor 'is all gorse now, flickering with flower; and then it will be heather; and then, hundreds of fox gloves'. It was, he concluded, 'the best place I have been in, I think'.

Country around Zennor, with the house where Lawrence stayed in the distance

These were vivid first impressions that never left him, and which he repeated in *Kangaroo*, where he recalled how at Zennor 'the Cornish night would gradually come down upon the dark, shaggy moors, that were like the fur of some beast, and upon the pale-grey granite masses, so ancient and Druidical'. And 'Cornish night' would be followed by 'A Cornish, magic morning', where walkers savouring the daybreak Zennor air 'passed the stony little huddle of the church-town, and on up the hill, where the great granite boulders shoved out the land, and the barrenness was ancient and inviolable'. Here they might 'see the gulls under the big cliffs beyond' or watch 'a buzzard circling over the marshy place below church-town'.

'I feel we ought to live here', he explained to the Murrys, 'pitch our camp and unite forces, and become an active power here, together'. He drew a little sketch-map to show the Murrys what Higher Tregerthen was like: 'One block has three cottages that have been knocked into one, and the end room upstairs made into a tower-room...Katherine would have the tower-room with big windows and panelled walls...rent will be very low and all is *perfectly lovely*'. The adjoining block, where Lawrence and Frieda would live, consisted of two cottages. Lawrence hoped that Philip Heseltine might also rejoin them, and that Emma could be persuaded to come from Porthcothan as housekeeper. It sounded idyllic: they would be 'like a little monastery...we will eat together in the dining-room of your house...[and] share expenses...It would be *so splendid* if it could but come off: *such* a lovely place: our *Rananim*'.

The moral pressure on the Murrys was now relentless. Three days later Lawrence wrote to the couple again. He and Frieda had taken their cottage at Higher Tregerthen for £5 a year, and 'Really, you must have the other place. I keep looking at it. I call it already, Katherine's house, Katherine's tower'. There will be no 'quarrels and quibbles', he insisted, and there would be a binding '*Blutbruderschaft* between us all'. Here Lawrence was proposing a yet deeper spiritual dimension to his search for *Rananim*, the stipulation that they should all become 'blood-brothers'. He had seen in the Zennor landscape suggestions of 'blood sacrifice', as he put it, part of the 'pregnant malevolency of Cornwall' which he found strangely and powerfully compelling. He had been attracted, as he admitted in *Kangaroo*, to 'the savage vibrations that still lingered round the secret rocks...old awful presences round the black moor-edge...the blood-sacrificial pre-world, and the sun-mystery, and the moon-power, and the mistletoe on the tree'. 'I am *Bludbruder*', Lawrence declared to the Murrys in almost menacing tones. But if the idea had alarmed Jack and Katherine, it did not

Higher Tregerthen – Katherine Mansfield's tower can be seen easily

prevent them from being seduced by Lawrence's purple prose and his passionate advocacy of the delights of Zennor. As Lawrence wrote to Katherine, 'we count you two as our only two *tried* friends, real and permanent and truly blood kin. I know we shall be happy this summer; so happy'.

Jack and Katherine arrived in early April 1916. 'The Murrys have come', Lawrence wrote eagerly to Ottoline Morrell on the 7th, 'and we are busy getting their cottage ready: colouring the walls and painting and working furiously...we all enjoy ourselves'. But the truth was that the Murrys were shocked by what they found. Although Jack avowedly enjoyed his long walks across the moors with Lawrence, he and Katherine found Lawrence a changed man – ill (the encroaching TB), and often angry and frustrated and ranting. And although Katherine wrote approvingly to her friend Virginia Woolf, explaining how she walked across the fields to collect bread from Katie Berryman, returning along the coastal footpath beside the bewitching Atlantic, she did not really take to the harsh, grey beauty of

Higher Tregerthen Cottage – photograph taken by Lawrence and sent
to his sister (Manuscripts and Special Collections, University
of Nottingham La R 4/6/5)

Our cottage is practically done. At last I am in my own home and feel content. I feel I have a place here. The cottage looks very nice. I made a dresser, with cupboard below, and shelves for the plates above, also bookshelves. These are painted royal blue, and the walls are a pale pale pink, and the ceiling with its beams is white. This is downstairs, a rather low, square room with thick walls. Upstairs looks really beautiful: a good-sized room with a large deep window looking to the sea, and another window opposite looking at the hill-slope of gorse and granite ... We have only these two rooms, and a long scullery-kitchen with sloping roof at the back. But it is quite enough, there is all the world outside, the sea and the moor-hills quite open.

Letter to Ottoline Morrell, 7 April 1916

Zennor and West Penwith. It was too bleak, and she complained that in damp weather the walls of her cottage ran with wet. This was not at all the romantic 'Katherine's tower' that Lawrence had led her to expect.

But far worse were the fights between Lawrence and Frieda. Katherine had decided she did not much like Frieda – she was a 'huge German pudding' – but nonetheless was appalled when it became apparent that Lawrence was beating her. 'Let me tell you what happened on Friday', Katherine wrote to a friend, 'I went across to them for tea. Frieda said Shelleys Ode to a Skylark was false'. Lawrence had lost his temper at this remark, and he and Frieda began to quarrel. 'Out of my house – you little God Almighty you', she cried, and Lawrence threatened that he would 'give you a dab on the cheek to quiet you, you dirty hussy'. At that point Katherine diplomatically slipped out to return to her own cottage. Later in the evening, Frieda turned-up to report that it was finally all over between her and Lawrence, and that she had left him for good. Then Lawrence himself appeared at the door. As Katherine continued:

Suddenly Lawrence appeared and made a kind of horrible blind rush at her and they began to scream and scuffle. He beat her – beat her to death – her head and face and breast and pulled out her hair. All the while she screamed for Murry to help her. Finally they dashed into the kitchen and round and round the table. I shall never forget how L[awrence] looked. He was so white – almost green and he just hit – thumped the big soft woman. Then he fell into one chair and she into another. No one said a word. A silence fell except for Frieda's sobs and sniffs...L. sat staring at the floor, biting his nails.

After fifteen minutes or so, astonishingly, Lawrence looked up and asked Jack a question about French literature. Slowly the atmosphere changed, and before long Lawrence and Frieda were swapping notes on the making of macaroni cheese! Next morning, a thoroughly chastened Lawrence could not do enough for Frieda. As Katherine observed, 'he was running about taking her up breakfast to her bed and trimming her hat'. Yet to this unsettling episode was soon added Lawrence's renewed approaches to Jack about *Bludbrudershaft*, the suggestion now being not so much an understanding between them all, the 'Lawrences' and 'Murrys' together, but – as Jack feared – perhaps some kind of secret, darker 'pre-Christian blood rite' to be performed out on the moors. It was all rather discomforting. Altogether, the Murrys endured it all for about six weeks, then moving to Mylor on the softer south coast of Cornwall, near Falmouth. Lawrence reported blandly to Ottoline, drawing a veil over the drama, explaining that 'Unfortunately the Murrys do not like the country – it is too rocky and bleak for them. They should have a soft valley, with leaves and the ring-dove cooing'. As he added to another friend, Barbara Low, writing on 30 May, 'the Murrys are going away in a fortnight. They have taken a house near Falmouth. The walls of their cottage are rather damp'.

Lawrence found it difficult to understand why he had repelled the Murrys, and he and Frieda later visited them at Mylor to ensure there were no hard feelings. Outwardly, relations were restored (although, alas, it seems likely that Katherine Mansfield had caught from Lawrence the tuberculosis that was shortly to kill her), and Lawrence could still claim – as he had written to Catherine Carswell in April – that 'in this queer outlandish *Celtic* country, I feel fundamentally happy and free'. But inwardly Lawrence was in despair. 'I have done with the Murries, both, for ever', he wrote to Kot on 7 November 1916, 'so God help me'. He continued: 'I tell you my *Rananim*, my Florida idea, was the true one. Only the people were wrong'.

As Lawrence half-admitted, it was apparent that the Cornish *Rananim* was not working out. After the initial difficulties at Porthcothan, here was a further debacle at Higher Tregerthen with the Murrys. But he was nothing if not tenacious, and he invited a string of other guests – including Catherine Carswell and Barbara Low – to stay in the cottage vacated by the Murrys and to experience something of his Cornish vision. Despite everything, he tried to keep the prospect of *Rananim* alive, and during 1917 his dreams received a boost when Cecil Gray, the Scottish composer and friend of Philip Heseltine, took a cottage at Bosigran, about three miles west of Higher Tregerthen. Heseltine was also on the scene, apparently having rekindled his friendship with Lawrence, although even as they patched things up Lawrence was busy depicting Heseltine and Puma as the

Katherine Mansfield, taken by Lady Ottoline Morrell 1916-1917
(NATIONAL PORTRAIT GALLERY, LONDON)

unsavoury characters 'Halliday' and 'Possum' in his new novel *Women in Love*. For a short time, Bosigran became the twin pole, along with Higher Tregerthen, of what was to prove the last ditch attempt to found *Rananim* in Cornwall. During those months Lawrence and Gray met almost daily, Lawrence even helping Gray with domestic chores at the cottage at Bosigran. Frieda took a special shine to Gray, who had something of a reputation as a 'lady's man', and in the summer of 1917 she began to walk across to Bosigran alone – for the purpose, it is said, of frequent love-making with the handsome young Scot. It was not surprising that Gray would later recall that summer as 'halcyon days without intermission'.

John Middleton Murry, taken by Lady Ottoline Morrell 1917
(National Portrait Gallery, London)

By this time, Lawrence had made another important friendship, with a local farmer, thirty-three year old William Henry Hocking, one of two brothers down at Lower Tregerthen. Initially, Lawrence lent a hand on the Hocking's farm, in the late summer of 1916 helping to bring in the harvest. As he explained to his friend Dollie Radford on 5 September, 'We have had outrageous seas, and of a dark, wine-blue colour. The bracken is withering, the sunsets are tremendous, almost terrible, the autumn is coming in'. But the harvest was not yet gathered. 'The corn stands in "mews" – small ricks, in the field – not carried yet. Of course, William Henry is behind. He has got half his cut yet. It must all be cut by scythe'. Lawrence liked helping out, enjoying the physical labour and being outdoors, and feeling that he was making himself useful. It also gave him his first real opportunity to get to know the Cornish on their own terms, as equals. They were still 'different', but now in a sensuous, seductive way that contrasted with his earlier estimate of the Cornish as 'insects gone cold'. William Henry, Lawrence told Dollie Radford on 11 October, had 'something manly and independent about him – and something truly *Celtic* – something non-Christian, non-European, but strangely beautiful and fair in spirit, unselfish'.

By 1917 Lawrence and William Henry had become close, and Lawrence may even have considered him a potential recruit for *Rananim*. Subsequently, Lawrence's several biographers have argued about the precise nature of the relationship between Lawrence and William Henry Hocking. The consensus appears to be, as Brenda Maddox has put it, that 'in the fine summer of 1917, lying in the bracken and talking about sex, Lawrence and Hocking consummated their love'. William Henry's younger brother, Stanley, always strenuously denied that Lawrence had any homosexual tendencies. But, significantly, Frieda was not so sure, and was inclined to believe the stories about Lawrence and William Henry. Years later she affected not to care but at the time the rumours had made her unhappy. Equally significantly, William Henry appears to have been Lawrence's model for the 'strange Cornish type of man' with 'dark, fine, rather stiff hair and full, heavy, softly-strong limbs' sketched in a Prologue written (but never published) for *Women in Love*, the novel he penned at Higher Tregerthen, a 'type of man' to whom Rupert Birkin, the book's main male character, was intensely attracted. Likewise, in his semi-autobiographical novel *Kangaroo*, Lawrence's *alter ego*, Richard Lovett Somers, lies in the Cornish countryside with a handsome young farmer, talking of 'the mysterious change in man with the change of season, and the mysterious effects of sex on a man'.

'The Nightmare'

WHATEVER THE DETAILS OF the relationship, D.H. Lawrence's intimate friendship with William Henry Hocking opened for him a new window onto Cornish life. The Cornish were no longer people to be observed from 'a motor', as they had been at Porthcothan, but now could be work colleagues and friends. He began to understand the interests and anxieties of the Zennor community, from following the seasonal rhythm of the farming year to sharing in local events. On 5 May 1917, for example, he wrote to Murry to report a local tragedy that had unsettled him. 'Annie Thomas, the washerwoman, had a son of sixteen years, illegitimate son of Willie Berryman. This selfsame son went and fell off the cliffs on Sunday, getting gulls' eggs, and is quite lost'. Somehow, Lawrence thought, this calamity was emblematic of a wider dread he had sensed in Cornwall. 'All the Cornish farmers are filled with the sense of inevitable disaster', he told Murry, and 'talk freely of the end of the world'.

The war was dragging on, with casualties continuing to mount on a scale unimaginable, and the stunning advances of the Germans' spring offensive in 1917, though underplayed in the press, had damaged civilian morale. The year before, in the aftermath of the Somme, Lawrence had written to Catherine Carswell to explain that 'These Cornish are most, most unwarlike, soft, peaceable, ancient. No men could suffer more than they, at being conscripted...This is the most terrible madness'. On 11 December 1916, he had written to Cynthia Asquith in similar vein. 'Over Cornwall, last Wednesday and Thursday, went a terrible wave of depression. In Penzance market, farmers went about with wonder-stuck faces'. 'We're beaten', they had told Lawrence, 'I'm afraid we're beaten. These Germans are a wonderful nation...more than a match for us'. As Lawrence had concluded: 'That is Cornwall at the present time'.

Lawrence knew well the dread experienced by the young men locally as they anticipated delivery of their call-up papers, the awful wait for the postman cycling across from St Ives with brown 'O.H.M.S. envelopes brimming in his bag. Lawrence empathised, because he had gone through it himself. As he wrote to Dollie Radford on 29 June 1916:

I have just come back from Bodmin. Yesterday I had to go and 'join the colours' in Penzance. They conveyed me to Bodmin – a distance of fifty or sixty miles. We were kept – thirty poor devils – in the barracks all night, and treated as incipient soldiers. Luckily I got a total exemption – and am home again. But it was a great shock that barracks experience – that being escorted by train, lined up on station platforms, marched like a criminal through the streets to a barracks. The ignominy is horrible, the humiliation...what a degradation and a prison, oh intolerable. I could not bear it – I should die in a week if they made me a soldier. Thirty men in their shirts, being weighed like sheep, one after the other – God!...I beg all my stars that I may never see Bodmin again. I hate it so much.

Again, this was an episode that Lawrence wove into *Kangaroo*, with Somers also forced to make the journey to Bodmin. Like Lawrence himself, he seemed 'pale, silent, isolated; a queer figure, a young man with a beard' – but not young enough to prevent other would-be recruits calling him 'Dad'. Like Lawrence, Somers 'never forgot that journey up to Bodmin, with other men who were called up. They were all bitterly, desperately miserable'. On the train to Bodmin, they had yelled tunelessly the words of 'I'll be your sweetheart, if you will be mine'. Now, Somers imagined, 'those ghastly melancholy notes' were 'Wailing down the lost corridors of hell'.

Like his *alter ego*, Lawrence felt as much for the other conscripts as he did for himself. After all, he had got his exemption – the presiding doctor immediately recognized his medical condition – but the others were on their inexorable journey to the trenches. 'I liked the men', he wrote to Catherine Carswell on 9 July 1916, 'They all seemed so *decent*...It was the underlying sense of disaster that overwhelmed me. They are all so brave, to suffer...so noble, to accept sorrow and hurt'. Lawrence was amazed at their acceptance of it all: 'they accepted it, as one of them said to me, with a wonderful purity of spirit – I could howl my eyes out over him – because "they believed first of all in their duty to their fellow man"'. On 1 September he was still expressing his irrepressible anger, writing to Cynthia Asquith: 'My blood cribbles with fury to think of it...The whole of militarism is so disgusting'.

In March 1917 Lawrence heard that, with the rules changed, he might be liable for call-up once more. But now he seemed past caring. He told all who might listen how pointless was the war and how he would not fight just because 'Germany invaded Belgium'. To those whose sons, fathers, brothers had dutifully gone off to war – and perhaps to their deaths – this began to sound a little precious, rather self-indulgent. The locals, many of whom had not warmed to Frieda's aristocratic manner, remembered that she was German – and a relation of the feared 'Red Baron'. They knew that the Lawrences had German newspapers sent to Higher Tregerthen (they came from Frieda's sisters, sent via Switzerland), and they did not know that the unintelligible Hebridean folk-songs sung so lustily when the Lawrences visited Cecil Gray at Bosigran were not German patriotic compositions. The Atlantic was close-by and Allied merchantmen were being sunk by U-boats in full sight of the Cornish coast. To make matters worse, Gray had been careless in observing the blackout, showing an unobscured light at night which, if not actually signally to enemy submarines (as some suspected), could be a useful navigational aid to any marauding U-boat. The police called on Gray, and subsequently, in early October 1917, he was fined twenty pounds for his misdemeanour – a substantial sum.

Far worse was to follow. On 11 October, while Lawrence was in Penzance with William Henry and Frieda was over at Gray's cottage at Bosigran, the police raided Higher Tregerthen. They had gone through Lawrence's correspondence and disturbed Frieda's work-basket. Coming so soon after the Cecil Gray incident, it was clear that there was now a whispering campaign against them, and that already Lawrence's affectionate embrace by the local farming community was being overshadowed by a wider suspicion and hostility. The very next day the raid was followed-up by a visit from an Army Major, together with a police-sergeant and two plain-clothes policemen. Lawrence was presented with a military order, signed by Major-General W. Western of Southern Command, Salisbury, informing him that he and Frieda had three days to quit Cornwall. Bewildered, Lawrence sat down to write to Cynthia Asquith. 'Now comes another nasty blow', he announced. 'The police have suddenly descended on the house, searched it, and delivered us a notice to leave the area of Cornwall'. He could not understand why, he protested, perhaps a little disingenuously. 'This bolt from the blue has fallen this morning', he wrote, 'why, I know not…We are as innocent even of pacifist activities, let alone spying of any sort as the rabbits in the field outside'. In the face of the mighty power of the State, which had caught up with and crushed the last vestiges of his *Rananim*, Lawrence was impotent. He had little choice but to obey the order, and he and Frieda began to pack their belongings.

Once more, it was an experience that Lawrence described in Kangaroo, in a chapter entitled 'The Nightmare'. Like Lawrence, Richard Lovett

Somers had fallen under the spell of Cornwall:

Cornwall is a country that makes a man psychic. The longer he stayed, the more intensely it had that effect on Somers. It was if he were developing second sight, and second hearing. He would go out into the blackness of night and listen to the blackness, and call, call softly, for the spirits, the presences he felt coming downhill from the moors in the night. 'Tuatha De Danaan!' he would call softly [invoking the pre-Christian Celtic gods]. 'Tuatha De Danaan! Be with me. Be with me'. And it was as if he felt them come.

Alas, despite this intimate embrace, the spell was ruined for Somers, as it was for Lawrence, by the further encroachment of England's war: 'The war-wave had broken right over England, now: right over Cornwall. Probably throughout the ages Cornwall had not been finally swept, submerged by any English spirit. Now it happened – the accursed later war spirit'. But the Cornish were tenacious and subversive, like all Celts, like David Lloyd George: 'A little Welsh lawyer, not an Englishman at all'. Somers (and Lawrence) approved of their duplicity: 'Somers gradually came to believe that all Jews, and all Celts, even whilst they espoused the cause of England, subtly lived to bring about the last humiliation of the great old England...Let the Celts work out their subtlety'. Somers listened as they 'spoke in the quick Cornish way' and he watched carefully 'their black eyes...Right and wrong was not fixed for them as for the English'.

Like Lawrence, Somers and his wife Harriet (for Frieda) were given the summary order to get out of Cornwall forthwith:

Somers, white and very still, spoke no word, but waited. Then the police-sergeant, in rather stumbling fashion, began to read an order from the military authorities that Richard Lovatt Somers and Harriet Emma Marianna Johanna Somers, of Trevetham Cottage, etc, should leave the county of Cornwall within the space of three days. And further, within the space of twenty-four hours of their arrival in any place they must report themselves at the police station of the said place, giving their address. And they were forbidden to enter any part of the area of Cornwall, etc, etc, etc.

'But why?' cried Harriet. 'Why? What have we done?'.

'I can't say what you have done', said the young officer in a cold tone, 'but it must be something sufficiently serious. They don't send out these orders for nothing'.

When Lawrence and Frieda left Cornwall, like the fictional Somers and Harriet, they made for London. William Henry Hocking drove them in his cart to the branch-line station at St Ives. An abrupt entry in his diary for 15 October 1917 was his only lasting commentary on his encounter with the great man: 'To St Ives – Lawrence'.

D.H. Lawrence 1915
(National Portrait Gallery, London)

'The Phoenix'

LAWRENCE CONTINUED TO INSIST that it was all a mistake, making enquiries as to how to reverse the decision. 'I very much want to be allowed to go back to Cornwall', he wrote to an official on 23 October, 'We have got the house there, and are rooted there'. He was quietly confident, as he told Cecil Gray six days later: 'These govt. people are the devil, with their importance and their "expediency" and their tyranny. But I believe we shall get back to Zennor next month'. Alas, it was not to be. In fact, for some time now Lawrence had known inwardly that he needed to get out of Britain altogether, to escape England's snare. As long ago as December 1916 he had told Catherine Carswell that 'I believe that England...is capable of seeing only badness in me, for ever and ever. I believe America is my virgin soil: truly'. Likewise, in January 1917, he had explained to Cynthia Asquith that he wanted 'to go far west, to California or the South Seas, and live apart, away from the world. It is really my old Florida idea – but one must go further west'. It was, he said to Catherine Carswell:

> *Time for us to go,*
> *Time for us to go...*

To his constant friend Kot, Lawrence wrote on 9 February 1917: 'We shall all come to our *Rananim* before many years are out – only believe me – an Isle of the Blest, here on earth. But the first thing is to cut clear of the old world – burn one's boats: if only one could'. In fact, he had tried to burn his boats, armed with his exemption from military service, and had applied for a passport to allow his once-and-for-all escape to America. But the authorities, with the intention of keeping a close eye on him, had rejected the request. For the duration of the war, he was grounded in the UK. Thereafter, let off the leash, Lawrence resumed his wandering, bringing him shortly to Australia, the principal setting for *Kangaroo*, first published in 1923.

Australia, as Lawrence well knew, had been a major destination for Cornish emigrants in the nineteenth century, part of a complex web that had taken Cornish men (mainly, but not exclusively, miners) and women to the four corners of the earth. This 'Great Emigration', as it was known, had created a Cornish transnational identity that, as Lawrence learned at Zennor, was still of considerable significance to local people. In the 1870s, for example, the closure of two small tin mines at Zennor had led to a mini exodus from the parish, accounting for a drop in its population from 600 to 500 in a decade and forging local family links with overseas communities as far distant as America and New Zealand. Earlier, in the 1850s, Cornish emigrants from Zennor had participated in the gold rush to Victoria in Australia. As one of them noted in a letter home, there on the Creswick diggings in 1854 were 'Richard Eddy from Treen and Matthew Thomas from Treen and David Eddy from Bosigran...Matthew White ... Richard Eddy from Bosigran, John Hosking from Treveal and Arthur Chellew from Zennor Church Town'.

In gaining his closer understanding of the Cornish at Zennor, not least by working in the fields with the farming families, Lawrence had begun to appreciate the importance of the emigration experience in moulding contemporary Cornish identity. His short-story 'Samson and Delilah', first published in 1922, drew upon a Cornish literary tradition of which Lawrence was clearly aware – the theme of the returned emigrant who, coming back to Cornwall after years abroad, is not recognised in his home village and finds everything much changed. In Lawrence's closely observed version of the story, a Cornish miner has come home to St Just-in-Penwith (not far from Zennor) from America. Arriving late at night, he goes to the local inn, 'The Tinners' Rest'. The returned miner is watched with interest by the landlady, Mrs Nankervis: 'She had noticed the man: a big fine fellow, well-dressed, a stranger. But he spoke with that Cornish-Yankee accent she accepted as the natural twang among the miners'. She also saw that he 'was handsome, well coloured, with well-drawn Cornish eyebrows, and the usual dark, bright, mindless Cornish eyes'. Yet she did not see that he was her husband, back from America at last, and the scene is set for a confrontation of passion and violence as the two are drawn into a strange, indifferent intimacy born of separate lives and all the years spent apart.

In going to Australia, and then on to other destinations across the globe in search of *Rananim*, Lawrence – consciously or unconsciously – had set himself in the role of the roving Cornish emigrant. In his writing, too, especially that published in the aftermath of the Great War, there is much evidence of the enduring influence of Cornwall and his Cornish days. *Kangaroo*, of course, is strongly autobiographical in parts, drawing upon Lawrence's Cornish 'nightmare'. *Women in Love* hints at his relationship with William Henry Hocking, and the novel's characters 'Halliday' and 'Possum' are only thinly disguised versions of Heseltine and Puma. In *The Fox*, one of Lawrence's several short novels, March, the heroine, marries a

Cornishman, Henry Grenfel, and goes to live in the west of Cornwall. There she experiences a self-emptying liberation not unlike that felt by Lawrence himself: 'there sitting in a niche of the high wild cliffs of West Cornwall, looking over the westward sea, she stretched her eyes her wider and wider. Away to the West, Canada, America . . .'. Elsewhere, there are other 'Celtic' traces in Lawrence's fiction, like the character Colin Urquhart in *The Princess* (another short novel) who is akin to 'some old Celtic hero'. *St Mawr*, Lawrence's story about a strong-willed race horse, is at one level a metaphor for the ancient struggle between Celt and Saxon.

During his relatively short time in Cornwall, Lawrence's view of the Cornish altered considerably. He had come to Cornwall armed with an array of English assumptions about 'the Celts' – some favourable, some not – and it is these colonialist prejudices that are often remembered today, especially in Cornwall itself. When Cornwall proved to be less immune to England's influence than he had hoped, with the Cornish passive in the face of coercion, Lawrence became angry. But at length he began to empathise with the Cornish, joining their community, and started to see the Celtic peoples as his natural allies, quietly subversive and duplicitous in their subtle attempts to undermine England's sway.

A.L. Rowse, the Cornish historian and man of letters, certainly felt much in common with D.H. Lawrence – because they shared a similar working-class, mining community background, together with a sense of overwhelming disappointment in the failure (as they saw it) of the workers to lift themselves from their narrow lives. Rowse was also sufficiently intrigued with the Tregerthen connection to write a short-story 'Night at the Carn', based on the strange death of Katherine Arnold-Foster, though moving the action away from Zennor to his own mid-Cornwall. Rowse was not alone in his obsession with Lawrence, and there remains today a lively and enduring literary fascination in Lawrence's Cornish sojourn. Helen Dunmore's acclaimed novel *Zennor in Darkness*, published in 1994, is a fictionalised account of Lawrence's time in Cornwall. More recently we have had John Worthen's BBC Radio 3 documentary 'Paradise or Nightmare? D.H. Lawrence in Cornwall', broadcast in May 2008, and Amy Rosenthal's well received play *On the Rocks* (about Lawrence, Frieda and the Murrys), first performed at the Hampstead Theatre in London in July 2008.

Today, there is no-one alive at Zennor who remembers D.H. Lawrence and his search for *Rananim* during the bleak years of the Great War. But when C.J. Stevens, an American writer of Cornish descent, visited Cornwall during the winter of 1967-68 to trace his Zennor ancestors, he found that Stanley Hocking – younger brother of William Henry – was living in retirement at nearby St Ives. Stevens soon won the confidence of the elderly Hocking, and was able to record a remarkable series of reminiscences about Lawrence, Frieda and their Zennor days. Towards the end of one interview session, Stanley Hocking suddenly asked his wife to go upstairs to fetch 'a metal box filled with yellowing newspaper clippings and what appeared to a glass-framed picture'. It was an astonishing moment. As Stevens explained, 'Hocking rose stiffly from his chair. "This is a little keepsake that Lawrence gave us Hockings", he said. It was a tapestry of the phoenix on its nest of flames. "Lawrence made this".'

Further Reading

Denys Val Baker, *The Timeless Land: The Creative Spirit in Cornwall*, Adams & Dart, Bath, 1973.

I. A. Copley, *The Music of Peter Warlock: A Critical Survey*, Dobson, London, 1979.

Robert Gathorne-Hardy, *Ottoline at Garsington: Memoirs of Lady Ottoline Morrell 1915-18*, Faber & Faber, London, 1974.

David Cox and John Bishop (eds.), *Peter Warlock: A Centenary Celebration*, Thames, London, 1994.

Sharon Lowenna, 'Noscitur A Sociis: Jenner, Duncombe-Jewell and their Milieu', in Philip Payton (ed.), *Cornish Studies: Twelve*, University of Exeter Press, Exeter, 2004.

Alan M. Kent, *The Literature of Cornwall: Continuity, Identity, Difference*, Redcliffe Press, Bristol, 2000.

Alan M. Kent, '"Song of our Motherland": Making Meaning of the Life and Work of Katharine Lee Jenner 1853-1936', in Derek R. Williams (ed.), *Henry and Katharine Jenner: A Celebration of Cornwall's Culture, Language and Identity*, Francis Bootle, London, 2004.

Brenda Maddox, *The Married Man: A Life of D.H. Lawrence*, Minerva, London, 1995.

Harry T. Moore (ed.), *The Collected Letters of D.H. Lawrence: Volume One*, Heinemann, London, 1962.

Julian Moynahan, 'Lawrence, Women and the Celtic Fringe', in Annie Smith (ed.), *Lawrence and Women*, Vision Press, London, 1980.

Paul Newman, *The Tregerthen Horror: Aleister Crowley, D.H. Lawrence and Peter Warlock in Cornwall*, Abraxas & DGR Books, n.p., 2005.

Philip Payton, *Cornwall: A History*, Cornwall Editions, Fowey, 2004.

Philip Payton, *A.L. Rowse and Cornwall: A Paradoxical Patriot*, University of Exeter Press, Exeter, 2005.

Philip Payton, *The Cornish Overseas: A History of Cornwall's Great Emigration*, Cornwall Editions, Fowey, 2005.

Philip Payton, 'John Betjeman and the Holy Grail: One Man's Celtic Quest', in Philip Payton (ed.), *Cornish Studies: Fifteen*, University of Exeter Press, Exeter, 2007.

Keith Sagar, *The Life of D.H. Lawrence: An Illustrated Biography*, Eyre Methuan, London, 1980.

C.J. Stevens, *Lawrence at Tregerthen*, Whitston, Albany (NY), 1988.

C.J. Stevens, *The Cornish Nightmare: D.H. Lawrence in Cornwall*, John Wade, Phillips (ME), 1996.

Claire Tomalin, *Katherine Mansfield: A Secret Life*, Penguin, London, 1988.

Ella Westland, 'D.H. Lawrence's Cornwall: Dwelling in a Precarious Age', *Cultural Geographies*, 9, 2002.

George J. Zytaruk, *The Quest for Rananim: D.H. Lawrence's Letters to S.S. Koteliansky 1914 to 1930*, McGill-Queen's University Press, Montreal & London, 1970.